The World Around Us

World Transport

travel & communications

Grolier Educational Corporation
SHERMAN TURNPIKE, DANBURY, CONNECTICUT 06816

How to use this book

There are many ways of using this book. Below you will see how each page is arranged to help you to find information quickly, revise main ideas or look for material in detail. The choice is yours!

On some pages you will find words that have been shown in CAPITALS. There is a full explanation of each of these words in the glossary on page 63.

This heading in the running text tells you about the section that follows.

This is the main column of running text that forms the chapter. Read this for a good understanding of the subject as a whole.

Scan these boxes for key ideas.

The information in the box describes an important subject in detail and gives additional facts.

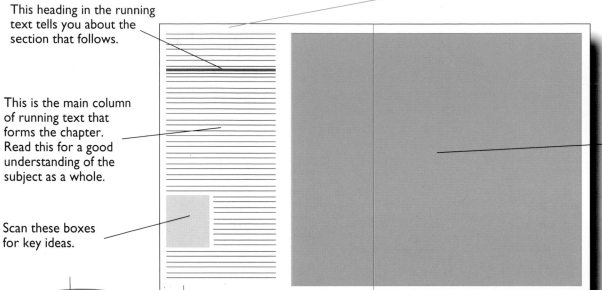

Author
Brian Knapp, BSc, PhD
Educational Consultant
Stephen Codrington, BSc, PhD
Art Director
Duncan McCrae, BSc
Editor
Elizabeth Walker, BA
Illustrator
David Woodroffe
Designed and produced by
EARTHSCAPE EDITIONS
Print consultants
Landmark Production Consultants Ltd
Printed and bound by
Paramount Printing Company Ltd

First published in the United States in 1994 by
Grolier Educational Corporation,
Sherman Turnpike, Danbury, CT 06816

Cataloging information may be obtained directly from Grolier Educational Corporation

ISBN 0–7172–7432–2

Acknowledgments
The publishers would like to thank the following for their help and advice: *Aspen Flying Club*, Englewood, Colorado; *Baramundi Air*, Cairns, Queensland; *Terry Barringer*, Royal Commonwealth Society Library, Cambridge University; *Bendigo Aviation Services*, Bendigo, VIC, Australia; *Bridgeford Flying Service*, Napa, California; *Matthew Cherian*, Oxfam-Bridge, India; *Eveland Aero*, Honolulu, Hawaii; *David Newell*, Oxfam-Bridge, Thailand and *Sonning Common Garage*.

Picture credits
(c=center t=top b=bottom l=left r=right)
All photographs are from the **Earthscape Editions** library except the following: **Jack Jackson** 15b, 60bl, 61br; **Panos Picture Library** 10/11 (*Hamish Wilson*), 42/43 (*Ron Giling*), 60br (*Liba Taylor*); **Royal Commonwealth Society Library** 18b, 22/23, 23cl; **The Sutcliffe Gallery** 19t; **University of Reading, Rural History Centre** 24t, 25tc (*Mrs Iris Moon, Sulham House, Sulham, Pangbourne, Berkshire*), 37cl; **Tony Waltham** 62tr; **ZEFA** 23tr, 27t, 37cr, 44bl.

This product is manufactured from sustainable managed forests. For every tree cut down at least one more is planted.

Contents

Chapter 1

Facts about transport

Transport is crucial to all our lives. In most industrial countries people spend a fifth of their incomes on transport, and about one worker in ten is employed in transport. We rely on all kinds of transport to get to work, visit the shops, travel to relatives or go on vacation to distant parts of the world. It is truly a central part of modern living.

The word *transport* comes from trans (across) and port (to carry). All modern countries put transport at the top of their priorities, but the cost of transport varies enormously from country to country. In part this depends on the number of people on the move. The more people move about, the cheaper transport can be. This is why transport costs in countries with large populations, like the United States for example, are among the lowest in the world.

Some countries help to keep the cost of transport low by paying for part of the real cost. This payment is called a subsidy. Subsidies are given to most city bus services, and many countries subsidize their trains as well. This is because buses and trains are thought of as public transport, that is, the transport that the public must have for their everyday needs. Air and sea transport, on the other hand, are almost never subsidized because they are seen as forms of travel that people can choose to do without.

⤒ (left) Transport plays a key role in all our lives. There is a wide choice of types of transport, each geared to suit a particular type of journey. Some forms of transport are uncommon, like these narrow double-decker streetcars that are as famous a part of Hong Kong roads as the streetcars of San Francisco or the red buses of London.

The importance of transport

You can gain a clear example of the importance of transport in our lives when you realize that people in industrial countries spend about a fifth of their entire income on traveling, buying vehicles and related activities.

> As countries become richer they turn from public to private transport, from rail to road. The change causes congestion and pollutes the environment.

All industrial world countries have large railway networks and ever-increasing volumes of airline passengers.

Transportation is also a national priority in all the DEVELOPING WORLD countries because all governments know that if businesses are to sell their goods, they must get the goods to the customers quickly and cheaply. However, the high cost of modern transport makes it difficult to introduce the improvements these countries would like.

Transport creates jobs

Transport is not just a means of getting around; it has given us a better way of life. But at the same time we have grown to depend on transport more and more for earning a living. Driving vehicles and running public transport systems have created the biggest manufacturing industry in the world.

The number of new vehicles coming onto the world's roads is fantastic. There are nearly 50 million new vehicles made each year in the world, of which 13 million are made in Japan, 10 million in the United States and 5 million in Germany.

Not surprisingly, those who work directly in transport and those who make vehicles comprise one fifth of the entire workforce of the industrial world. This means that making vehicles, building and repairing roads, running

How transport works

Cost, convenience and time influence transport and travel today even more than in the past. There is still no single means of transport that will be suited to every travel need, no single best way of carrying ourselves and our goods wherever we want to go.

In many ways we use transport in exactly the same way as our ancestors, who, thousands of years ago, decided to use rivers to carry their cargoes rather than to walk overland. They would have brought perhaps hides and dried meat to the river's edge, loaded them onto canoes drawn up on a bank and then paddled off to trade with other people along the river.

Today the process may seem much more complicated, but the same ideas are involved. Travel and transport still require:
- A means of transport (barge, aircraft, train, etc.);
- A network of routes to travel on (canal, railway line, road, etc.);
- A place to move from one route to another or from one kind of transport to another (airport, dock, railway station, etc.);

and because many people are involved in moving, the whole system of public travel and transport also requires
- A way of controlling traffic (air traffic control, railway signals, traffic lights, bus timetables, etc.).

The cost of public and private transport
Although people often think public transport is expensive, the cost of public travel by air, rail or bus is about a third of the cost of using a private vehicle. This is because people are *sharing* the cost of the transport.

Yet despite the low cost of travel by public transport, about two thirds of all journeys in industrial countries are by private car.

Customers moving freight have to balance the cost of speedy delivery with the cost of their goods. The cheapest form of transport is to send bulk low-value cargoes, such as oil, by barge. In comparison, sending the same weight of goods over the same distance by pipeline would cost 25 percent more; sending it by rail would be 4 times as costly, 18 times as costly by truck and nearly 1,500 times as much if the same cargo was sent by air freight.

Start of journey

Decide on the most suitable form of transport. Choose between speed, cost and fragility.

Air?

Road?

Sea?

Pipeline?

Rail?

Find a suitable route through the network of choices.

Port, railway station, etc.

Route

Destination

railways, operating airports and building cargo and passenger ships is a central part of our lives.

Exporting vehicles is one of the major items of trade in the industrial world. So when, for example, the vehicle industry suffers from lack of orders – as it did in the early 1990s – this has a huge impact on jobs and prosperity throughout the world.

> The greater the speed and care taken in moving people or goods, the more expensive transport becomes.

The result of our love affair with transport is that today most countries simply cannot afford to stop making cars, building new roads and encouraging people to travel. If the transport industry became smaller permanently, there would be severe unemployment. The fact is that the world has become hooked into a transport spiral from which there seems no obvious way out.

Governments pay the bills

Even ancient civilizations were keen to develop their transport systems. The Romans, for example, whose empire was at its height two thousand years ago, were experts at route planning. They supported their transport systems, using taxes to pay for harbor improvements, to build roads and to research into road, vehicle and transport systems, just as governments do today. Governments also support transport through the enormous amounts of money that they spend on military vessels, aircraft and vehicles.

Most countries have national road, rail and canal networks. Many airports are also government owned. Governments get the money for their transport schemes in part from taxes on vehicles and fuel. Throughout the world, governments have also passed special laws and given special benefits to allow highways, canals and railways to be built.

Transport to and from cities

Transport has had a dramatic effect on cities. Mass transport has allowed people to live farther from their work and still have short journey times. Improvements to mass transport were directly responsible for the sprawl of the city: without rapid transport (whether it be streetcars, buses, suburban railways or underground railways) the word SUBURB would never have needed to be invented and cities would have remained cramped, airless places.

Good communication has often meant life or death to a city. It would have made no sense for people in the ancient world to have built a city anywhere other than on a coast or a navigable river. As the 18th- and 19th-century INDUSTRIAL REVOLUTION got under way it would have been unthinkable to develop an industry at a place where there was no railway, and in the 20th century no city could survive if was not at a major junction of motorways or at a port.

❐ (above) Travel has brought many benefits, but it has also brought its share of problems. For example, in almost all countries better transport has allowed people to live much farther from their work than they used to. But as they COMMUTE each day between their homes and their workplaces they cause CONGESTION.

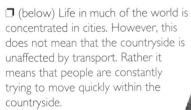

(above) The city has many types of activity, and each has its own special transport needs. In this picture you can see the spread of industry in the foreground; it needs highways that can handle large trucks. By contrast the city center (shown by the skyscrapers) needs to be able to cope with large numbers of commuters arriving and departing by car or public transport.

(below) Life in much of the world is concentrated in cities. However, this does not mean that the countryside is unaffected by transport. Rather it means that people are constantly trying to move quickly within the countryside.

Some of the places most affected are older countryside settlements whose roads are too narrow to cope with the amount of modern traffic. The only sensible solution to the plight of such places is to divert traffic around them by building a bypass. Bypasses are a natural result of building intercity motorways.

(above) Increasing city transport can adversely affect the environment. More vehicles mean more traffic jams and noisier environments. More and more people are using motorized transport to help them with their journeys. But each additional vehicle adds to air pollution: through carbon dioxide, which is making the Earth warmer (the **GREENHOUSE EFFECT**); through **ACID RAIN** containing sulphur and nitrogen oxides that harm plants and water animals; through **OZONE**, that causes breathing problems; and often through the release of lead and other metals that cause illness and brain damage. Solving pollution problems has high priority in many countries so that we can all enjoy the benefits of better transport.

Choosing a transport system

Which kind of transport people rely on depends on the size of the country, its landscape, the wealth of its people and government priorities. For example, large countries will have more need for aircraft and railways than small ones; a mountainous country will find it impossible to use water transport; a country with limited money will often find roads cheaper to build than railways or airports. In a country where people are wealthy, many choose to travel by road and air. In the less-well-off countries people are more likely to use public transport, such as coaches or trains.

Transport has played a vital role in exploring new lands, holding them together and defending them from attack.

The CIS (Commonwealth of Independent States, the former USSR), for example, has some money for large projects but the people are relatively poor. It built a railway system from Moscow to the Pacific coast at the start of the 20th century to deliver military supplies to its army. Now people rely almost entirely on the railway network to get from city to city. With nearly 160,000 miles of track, it is the world's largest railway network. Few people travel by air or by car because they do not have the money. The nation's highways have been neglected, so even traveling by bus between cities is inconvenient.

By contrast, most people in the United States have turned to cars as a convenient way of getting around. Nearly everyone has a car, and many families have more than one. As a result, the railways are poorly used: the United States is not even in the top fifty users in the world railway league.

Transport for defense

Transport is not just a way of getting around, it is a way of holding countries together and of protecting them in times of attack. The Romans knew the power of routes and spent huge amounts of time and effort on their roads. These were not civil roads but military roads aimed at helping armies reach trouble spots and supplying forts on their boundaries.

A thousand years after the collapse of the Roman Empire, the British Empire stretched around the world, the largest empire the world has ever known. The way that the British navy controlled the sea lanes allowed them to keep control of their empire and protect it from others.

In the 19th century, the United States government spent a great deal of money supporting the railroads because a transcontinental railway system was vital to hold the country together. In fact, the proper name for the main United States highway network is the National Interstate *and Defense* System.

The cost of military transport

Military transport needs ships, aircraft and land vehicles that can stand up to fire power in a battle. They have to be built to very different standards from ordinary forms of transport. This makes them extremely expensive.

Military needs can sometimes take up enormous sums of money, making it difficult for countries even as large as the United States to find the money for other tasks. One cause of the breakup of the former USSR was the fact that the country could no longer afford its vast military.

Developing world countries

The world is a very unstable place, and in many developing world countries power struggles are commonplace. Governments fight rebels in a situation where both sides have limited experience of organization for war.

In these circumstances the transport links are vital. Developing world countries often have few rapid transport links, and the government has to try to defend them while the rebels try to disrupt them.

Governments find it easier to keep control in the cities, while the rebels find it easier to control the countryside. In general governments have little use for aircraft because the rebel troops tend to be scattered. Instead they prefer tanks because they can move over roads that have been blown up and across rough countryside. Otherwise troops are moved by road.

Major military powers

The world consists mainly of small national armies rather than major military powers. They have little need for long-distance transport. By contrast, the major powers use their military to fight battles worldwide. They need to be able to get troops and firepower quickly to wherever it is needed.

To achieve this the military uses a combination of navy, army and air force. Naval ships provide offshore platforms for strike planes and mobile stores of equipment. The air force has fast fighter-bombers that can strike and return to distant airfields. The army moves troops quickly using a variety of fast-tracked vehicles as well as tanks. In the Gulf War of 1991 the main ground successes involved tanks.

❏ (left) This picture shows an aircraft carrier being loaded with stores.

❏ (below) This picture was taken during the Somali civil war. Roads are few and far between and they are poorly surfaced. Battles were on a small scale – skirmishes – and between small groups.

Chapter 2

Revolutions in transport

Modern travel is so fast and easy that it is difficult to imagine how much effort has been put into taming the landscape for our convenience. The changes that have been made to transport are nothing short of revolutions, and as each revolution took place it also changed everyone's lives. Here are some of the most important historical steps that occurred.

Ancient civilizations did not have the benefit of modern means of transport; people had to find their own way across the land, and they often traveled over the same paths. In this way they created the world's first footpaths.

People can travel some remarkable distances on foot – even over rough ground. An average person can travel at about 1 mile an hour over rough ground on long journeys (including rests) and so will travel about 10 miles in a ten-hour day. This doesn't seem very much at first, but at this rate a person could cross a continent in a few months.

Besides transporting themselves, people often had to carry goods from one place to another. Carrying packs is tiring work; it is likely, therefore, that animals such as the cow, the elephant,

❑ (left and above) Aircraft, such as the huge jumbo jets like the one on the left, are now as common a sight as stagecoaches were in the 18th century or steam trains (like the one above) a century ago. However, cities have often found great difficulty in keeping up with the changes, especially finding room for airports!

the camel and the horse were tamed (domesticated) as much for carrying people and cargo as for providing meat, milk and hides.

Some animals carried panniers (bags) on their backs and others pulled simple sleds. However, sleds are not efficient ways of carrying goods; it took the invention of the wheel to revolutionize transport.

The wheel and roads

Of all the revolutions in transport, none has been as important as the invention of the wheel 5,000 years ago.

The first people to use simple wagons and carts lived in the Middle East and China. But a wheeled vehicle could not follow the narrow tracks that people and animals had previously used. So the wheel created the need for roads.

> Even simple roads allowed merchants and armies to travel up to four times as fast as when they walked over rough ground.

Early roads were not especially smooth by today's standards, although the best (such as the Roman roads) were surfaced with stone and soil. However, roadways allowed the average speed of horse- or camel-drawn carts to increase dramatically, from 2 miles/hr over unmade surfaces to perhaps 5-6 miles/hr on stone-surfaced roads.

Roads and empires

Empires and nations are held together by good communications, and a first-class road network was just as essential in the past as it is today.

The need for transport has always been driven by the demands of trade and defense. Merchants needed to get their wagon loads of merchandise from where it was made to the customers; army commanders needed to march armies quickly if they were to defend the borders of their land.

The earliest forms of transport

The constant tread of feet over the landscape will soon wear away the plants and leave a trail. Once this has happened the rough surface made by the plants will be trodden down into a smoother surface of soil. This is the way the first tracks were made and the way that many tracks across the countryside are preserved.

Some of the trails that people now walk on for pleasure may be thousands of years old. In some countries, such the United Kingdom, these ancient trails and tracks are preserved by law as public footpaths.

In places where the trails are in heavy use, people are continually passing one another side by side. In this way they tread a wider path. Indeed, in some cases the trail is so wide that it may be difficult to believe that it was not built on purpose.

Tracks and trails that have no surface stone or other hard material are called unimproved trails. They get very muddy and often impassable during wet times of the year. It is easier for an unimproved trail to be useful in a desert region where rainfall is sparse as opposed to a region where rain is common. So the wetter parts of the world were among the first to develop all-weather roads with improved surfaces.

❏ (below) In mountainous countryside such as in the Himalayas, the main means of transport is still by foot and pack animals. Building roads in such areas would be far too expensive. However, for those who live there the lack of modern transport produces great isolation and often great hardship as well.

(below) Where a trail had to cross a stretch of marshy ground, such as near a river, stones, logs and even sacks of wool or moss were laid across the trail. Traffic eventually pressed all this material into the ground and thus the crossing was given foundations. More logs were laid on top and wired together to hold them in place. This gave the crossing its surface.

None of this could be called road improvement because riding over the logs gave many a jolt. Indeed, the many ups and downs over these crossings earned them the nickname Corduroy roads, after the ridged cloth of the same name.

(above) It is easy to see how trails can be established by looking at a landscape that attracts many walking tourists. The problem facing the people who try to preserve the landscape is that trails become wider and wider with time as people seek a dry route in wet weather when the worn track becomes muddy.

(below) Traditional routes across hilly lands were made by generations of travelers wearing down the land to make a track. In many cases a modern dirt road suited to vehicles can be made simply by pulling a metal blade along the trail, using a machine called a grader. This trading track in Afghanistan is thousands of years old. It is still rare to find any vehicles on it.

Roads require planning, investment and maintenance, so only the most developed ancient civilizations were able to build roads. For this reason the biggest and best engineered road networks were found in the Persian, Greek and (most outstandingly of all) the Roman and Chinese empires.

The first surfaced roads

By the 17th and 18th centuries, Europe had become one of the most important regions of the world, but no European country had good means for land transport. The lack of surfaced roads made traveling extremely difficult. In wet conditions it became almost impossible.

Travel on unsurfaced routes was very slow and hazardous at any time. Important highways had to be up to a quarter-mile wide simply so that, in wet weather, drivers could find a route through the ever-widening quagmire of the unsurfaced route.

Horse-drawn stagecoaches would take days to complete relatively short distances, and passengers would have to sit in unheated conditions.

> Well-surfaced roads are the key to trade. But they cost so much that only governments can afford to build and maintain them.

The terrible nature of traveling in the days before proper roads can best be appreciated through the stories of the time. Those on the cold and wet outside seats of the stagecoach often used to fortify themselves with alcohol, and they sometimes fell off the tops of coaches while drunk. Cases were commonly reported where drunken passengers landed facedown in a deep water-filled carriage rut and drowned before they could be rescued!

The terrible condition of the roads is the reason most trade was by ship. In the early years of the 19th century it still cost as much to carry coal overland in the United States to

Road improvers

The first road improvers were the Romans. Their roads were built with drainage to either side and good foundations. But when the Roman Empire collapsed in the 5th century, the technique of road building was lost as well.

The first road improvers to herald in the roads of the modern age were local government officials in Hertfordshire, England. In 1633 they were allowed to charge tolls to pay for road improvements on the London to York road. But it took two centuries before roads with good waterproof surfaces and strong foundations would be widespread. Until this happened road transport simply could not become important.

❏ (below) An oxcart. This local transport of goods was usually all that could be managed when roads were poor.

(left) The heavy wear of iron-rimmed wheels and horses' hooves cut deep ruts in the roads. For this reason there were many road improvements beginning in the 18th century. This road has a stone and soil surface bound with oil.

Because the roads were slow to travel on, stops had to be frequent; inns were a regular feature along popular routes.

(right) Distance posts were introduced so that people could tell how far they had come and how much journey was left. The journey to London shown on this milepost would take many days by horse and carriage.

(left) Roman roads were a shining example of good technology. The road had a firm base made of stones and a slope so that rain water ran to the sides. The surface was made smooth by filling the space between the stones with pebbles and soil.

This Roman road runs straight across the moorland of northeast England. It is still in good condition two thousand years after its construction. The surface appears rough simply because, over the centuries, the soil and small stones that were packed between the large foundation stones have been washed away. It would not take a lot of effort to bring the road back into usable condition!

(above) To pay for the upkeep of roads, tolls were charged. The toll would be paid at a booth like this one. The road gates were opened only when the toll had been paid. The original roads were barred by long staffs, like pikes, that had to be lifted or turned to allow carts to pass. Hence they came to be known as turnpike roads.

Philadelphia from Richmond (about 270 miles) as it did to carry it by ship from Newcastle, England (about 4,490 miles).

Thus, many people lived by the coast or on navigable rivers (see page 20). But a country that is confined to riverbanks and coasts is unable to make use of most of its land, so if overland trade were to be feasible, land travel had to be improved.

The earliest good roads were made by private companies that charged tolls. Such toll roads – called turnpikes when they were invented in England in the 18th century – form the basis of the modern highway systems of many countries. In the United States toll roads are still called turnpikes. Other names for fast through-roads or superhighways (some of which are free, others toll roads) include expressway, freeway and motorway.

Sail, paddle and ships

While the road system on land was difficult and expensive, travel by water was relatively easy. So for many centuries people preferred to live near the coast or by a navigable river rather than inland.

> It used to be so much easier to travel by water than by land that most people traditionally settled by the coast or on large navigable rivers where they could use boats.

One of the earliest world civilizations, the Ancient Egyptians, did not use roads to keep their empire together at all. Rather, because their empire contained the great natural waterway of the Nile, they relied on boats.

Water transport must have been well known to all the ancient worlds, but to make use of it people had to be near the sea or navigable waterways. Rafts may have been the earliest way of transporting by water, perhaps by tying logs together and using the natural currents to carry the raft downstream.

Trade and the age of sailing

Although there are no "roads" at sea, most ships followed much the same routes between ports across the world. Sometimes, such as between America and Asia or America and Europe, ships were able to go by the most direct route, known as a GREAT CIRCLE ROUTE. But there would be many reasons for not following the shortest path. In winter, for example, ships might sail into a region of dangerous icebergs if they took the short route across the Atlantic.

The shortest *time* between ports was not always the shortest distance between them. Ships' captains made use of the seasonal winds to make good time. The main shipping routes thus lay along the path of the great prevailing wind bands that cover the Earth. The most reliable are the northeast and southeast winds that blow from midlatitudes toward the equator. They are known as the trade winds, because they carried trading sailing ships across the oceans.

Captains always tried to avoid the main becalming areas of the world such as the doldrums near the equator.

As soon as trade routes had been opened from Europe to the far East via the southern tip of Africa (the Cape of Good Hope) and to the Americas across the Atlantic, the amount of trade grew considerably and Europe in particular began a period of great prosperity. The large cargo ships they used to carry the goods were called galleons in the 17th century and East Indiamen in the 18th and 19th centuries. They could carry between 1,000 and 2,000 tons each.

❐ (below) For hundreds of years the junks of Chinese origin plied the eastern seas. They were made in many sizes, from the smallest coastal vessel to giant transport ships and warships. They were the fastest and most flexible forms of sailing ship for many centuries.

(above) Sailing ships were responsible for developing world trade. Two-masted ships, like the one shown here unloading coal, carried the bulk of coastal traffic. The bigger, three-masted Packet Boats were capable of traveling across the world with cargo even though they were small vessels by modern standards.

(left) Sailing ships are still extensively used in the Indian Ocean and the China Sea, mainly for carrying general cargoes between coastal ports. This is the old area of the port of Dubai in the Middle East. Triangular-sailed *dhows* are most common in the Indian Ocean; the square-sailed Chinese Junk is still common in the China Sea.

(above) This statue of Captain Cook looks out from his native North Yorkshire (from which he began his worldwide travels) across the North Sea. The pioneering travels of people like Cook opened up trading routes across the world.

Many nations became famous for their seafaring. The Arabs, in particular, sent their ships to trade along the coast of Africa and India and even got as far as Indonesia.

Largely, however, ocean navigation was difficult. Ships were mainly confined to coastal waters until the invention of the compass and the rudder about a thousand years ago. These inventions led to the construction by Europeans of the famous three-masted ships that carried Christopher Columbus to the Americas and James Cook to the South Seas.

Sailing ships were cheap to run but they were very dependent on a fair wind. In some parts of the world, where winds were poor or fitful, ships could find themselves becalmed for weeks. If trade was to grow, there had to be a more reliable way of powering ships. In fact, the great revolution for ships and boats relied on exactly the same invention that caused a revolution in land transport: the invention of the steam engine.

Steam

The steam engine was probably the most important transport invention after the wheel and the sail. It provided a reliable source of power far greater than wind or animals could provide. For this reason it not only allowed more goods to be carried, it allowed them to keep to a reliable timetable as well.

> Steam power meant that more goods could be carried more cheaply, quickly and reliably. This was vital to the success of the Industrial Revolution.

But to begin with people had to get used to how to work the steam engine. Early engines were not very efficient; they were bulky and heavy. They used enormous amounts of fuel, either wood or coal. This meant that they were quite unsuited to replacing the horse and cart. They were, however, very suitable for ships.

The first canals and the Industrial Revolution

Canals were a way of improving inland navigation that had first been developed by the Chinese in the 7th century. But their main development came in the early days of the 18th-century Industrial Revolution when the greater output of the new factories could only be managed by using water transport.

To tow barges along a canal there must be only a very gentle current. Rivers were too fast for barge traffic until the invention of the lock.

The most famous of the early canals were those developed in the United Kingdom in the 18th century because they were vital to the success of the Industrial Revolution. The boats, which could carry only twenty tons or so (half the capacity of a modern truck), were regarded as giants at the time. To reduce the size of the excavation needed for a canal, and to keep down the amount of water lost by each lock, long thin boats were designed, called narrow boats.

Canals of this size soon became obsolete when railways were invented, but larger canals are still important today.

❏ (above) Some lowland rivers could be made navigable by building weirs to increase the depth of water and to reduce the current. Barges could then make their way past the weirs through locks (see on the left of the picture). All such navigable waterways needed a towing path (now usually called a towpath) so that people or horses could walk along the bank and tow the barges.

Canal makes a sweeping curve to keep along a contour line.

Industrial village grows alongside the canal.

Industrial Revolution factory takes in iron ore from canals and sends out iron products.

❏ (below) A canal and factory in the Black Country region of England, one of the earliest sites of the Industrial Revolution.

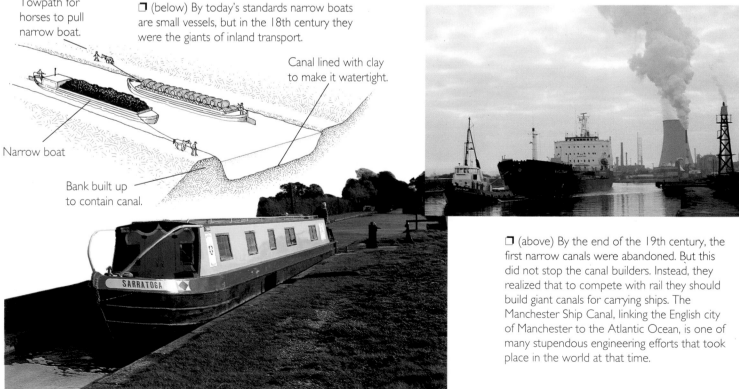

Towpath for horses to pull narrow boat.

❏ (below) By today's standards narrow boats are small vessels, but in the 18th century they were the giants of inland transport.

Canal lined with clay to make it watertight.

Narrow boat

Bank built up to contain canal.

SARRATOGA

❏ (above) By the end of the 19th century, the first narrow canals were abandoned. But this did not stop the canal builders. Instead, they realized that to compete with rail they should build giant canals for carrying ships. The Manchester Ship Canal, linking the English city of Manchester to the Atlantic Ocean, is one of many stupendous engineering efforts that took place in the world at that time.

The greater maneuverability of the steamship, its independence of the weather and eventually its iron hull allowed ships to be bigger and therefore carry goods more economically.

Steam-powered vessels could be adapted in many ways. Many flat-keeled steamboats were built for large rivers such as the Mississippi where fast currents meant that sailing vessels were impractical. Indeed, it was the steamboat, and in particular its use on the Mississippi and its tributaries, that allowed people to begin to open up the American West.

Steam power came to be seen as having vital importance in land travel, and the steam engine was directly responsible for the invention of the steam train, or locomotive.

Locomotives and rail

Steam engines created an entirely new way of traveling. This was crucial to the success of the Industrial Revolution. The locomotive, its wagons, carriages and track created a huge demand for iron, steel and engineering skills.

Steam railways provided the first efficient means of travelling inland that the world had ever seen.

At the same time it made the movement of raw materials and finished goods so much cheaper that more and more people could afford to buy them.

The public railway began in 1825 with the 19-mile-long Stockton and Darlington Railway in northeast England. This cargo route was designed to carry coal from near the mines to ships waiting at the coast. Within a year it had been matched by the world's first passenger-carrying service between Liverpool and Manchester in northwest England.

The story of the development of steam railways is one of the most extraordinary in history. The speed at which railway track was laid and engines produced was nothing short

Railways open up new lands

Railways are a unique, and at first sight improbable, form of transport. A huge heavy locomotive has to haul itself and wagons or carriages along rails fixed in a track. A locomotive cannot go up or down very steep grades, and it cannot take sharp curves. Thus, the tracks have to be fairly straight and level.

These restrictions mean that tracks have to be carried over valleys on vast expensive viaducts and through hills in even more expensive tunnels. Yet despite all these disadvantages, railways revolutionized the world because once built they were fast and reliable and they actually made money.

The first railways were built where they were most needed for the Industrial Revolution. Passengers were not the main consideration. Instead railways were first built to haul coal and iron ore, girders and all manner of other industrial raw materials and goods. Today this is still their main activity.

People needed coaxing onto trains. There was no tradition of moving between cities because it had only previously been possible by using slow and expensive stagecoaches, so few people felt the need to travel. The railways changed this by offering low fares and getting government support.

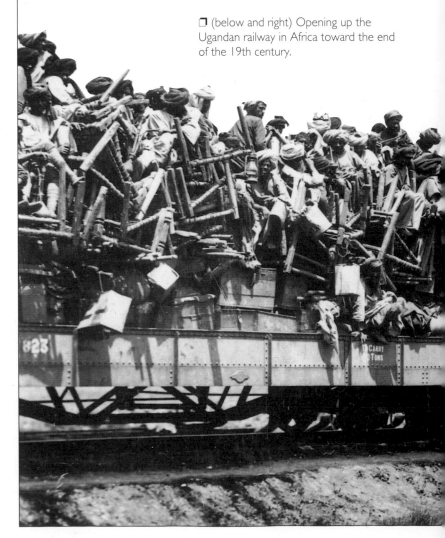

❐ (below and right) Opening up the Ugandan railway in Africa toward the end of the 19th century.

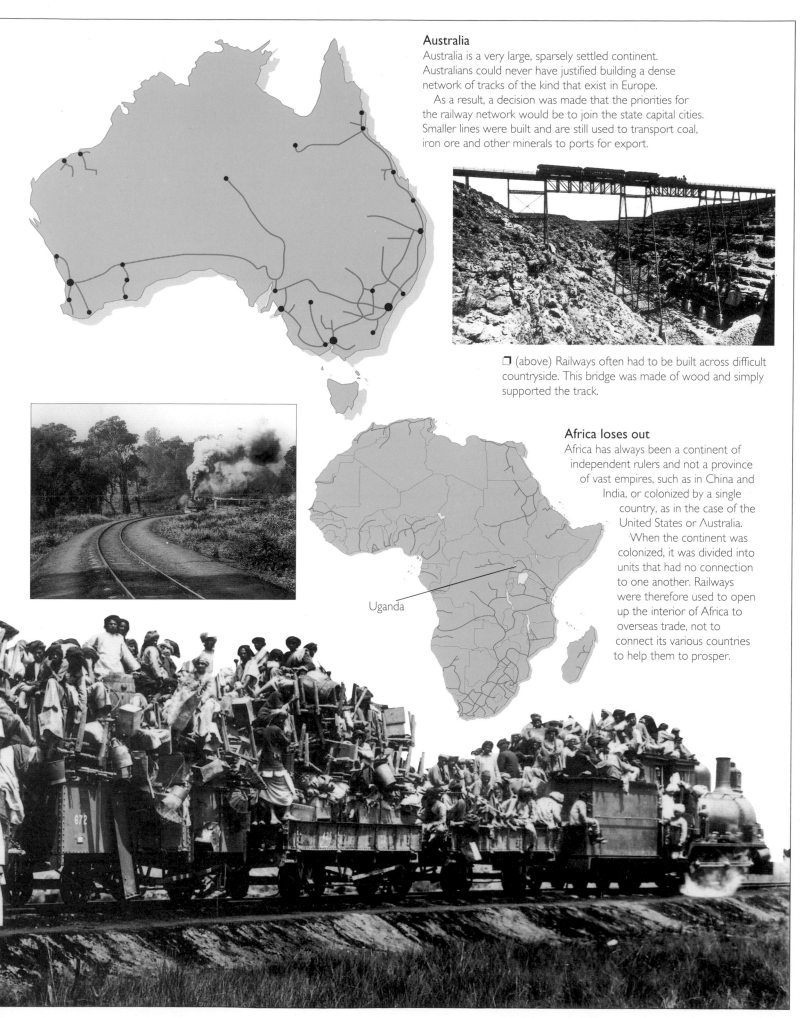

Australia

Australia is a very large, sparsely settled continent. Australians could never have justified building a dense network of tracks of the kind that exist in Europe.

As a result, a decision was made that the priorities for the railway network would be to join the state capital cities. Smaller lines were built and are still used to transport coal, iron ore and other minerals to ports for export.

❏ (above) Railways often had to be built across difficult countryside. This bridge was made of wood and simply supported the track.

Africa loses out

Africa has always been a continent of independent rulers and not a province of vast empires, such as in China and India, or colonized by a single country, as in the case of the United States or Australia.

When the continent was colonized, it was divided into units that had no connection to one another. Railways were therefore used to open up the interior of Africa to overseas trade, not to connect its various countries to help them to prosper.

Uganda

of phenomenal. Within fifteen years the industrial world had been turned from the age of animals to the age of machine power, through the laying of hundreds of thousands of miles of track.

Wherever the railway went, prosperity seemed to follow; wherever it missed seemed to fall into decline.

The railway was vital to factory owners because it could carry goods faster and get to places the canal builders had been unable to reach. But the railway also provided the ideal means of reaching into the interior of continents for the first time. As a result, by far the largest lengths of track were laid across the (then) unpopulated centers of the continents.

> The heroic task of building transcontinental railways in Russia and North America during the Railway Age was equivalent to the effort needed to put people on the moon during the Space Age.

At the same time cities were experiencing enormous congestion, and underground railways seemed the answer. These were at first powered by coal, which caused great pollution.

With the invention of electricity, however, the underground railway locomotives could be made pollution free. Today most major cities in the world have an underground railway system.

The motor age

Steam power was responsible for the success of the Industrial Revolution, yet its lifetime was to be little more than a century. The internal combustion engine, which displaced the steam engine at the end of the 19th century, relies on petroleum rather than steam. Its real advantage was in the power that could be gained from a lightweight engine.

Adapting to the motor vehicle

The first motor vehicle appeared in the 1890s. In 1914 Henry Ford adopted mass production because of the high demand. By the 1920s most American families had a car and a main national highway network was being built. Now there are around 230 million vehicles in the United States.

Although in other countries the rise of the motor vehicle was less spectacular, throughout the world the number of cars is booming and life and the environment are having to adapt to it. But at the same time, the motor vehicle is adapting to the changing world by becoming more fuel efficient, containing more recyclable materials and being more compact.

❏ (above) For thousands of years people traveled using animal power. As a result, a fifth of all farmland had to produce the fodder these animals required. Even so, horses, the most powerful draught animals, could still only travel short distances and pull relatively light loads. On long journeys horses had to be changed regularly or they would become too tired to move on. (The term *stagecoach* meant a passenger carriage that went in stages from one change of horses to another.)

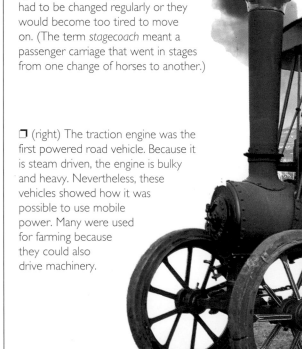

❏ (right) The traction engine was the first powered road vehicle. Because it is steam driven, the engine is bulky and heavy. Nevertheless, these vehicles showed how it was possible to use mobile power. Many were used for farming because they could also drive machinery.

❏ (right and below) Motorcars have changed design constantly this century. At first the car was built literally in the style of a horseless carriage (as in the picture on the right) just to allow people to get about.

People soon began to measure their wealth by the size and power of their cars. This was the age of the gasguzzlers (as in the picture below) when no thought was given to fuel consumption.

As fuel became more expensive, more thought was given to efficient engines, streamlining and lighter vehicles. People are now finding more uses for their cars, using them for carrying goods such as shopping as well as for getting around. This has led to the development of the hatchback and stationwagon.

❏ (above) Many of the old roads were not designed for motor vehicles. Roads can be widened in the countryside, but country villages and their narrow lanes often cause bottlenecks. The only solution is to build bypasses.

❏ (right) The suburbs are designed entirely around the motorcar. The car has clearly been the most important feature of city life from influencing the width of the roads to the need for garages beside each house.

Notice how the street pattern is designed both for local traffic (in the foreground) and for through traffic (the multilane highway in the background).

Without the car this kind of housing pattern would never have been invented.

The motor vehicle began as a horseless carriage in the 1890s. Within a decade Henry Ford had produced the Model T, the motor vehicle that was to make road transport dominate over all others. And it was the need for more and more such vehicles that encouraged Henry Ford to invent the mass-production system, now so widely used in industry.

Whereas the railway was invented and developed first in Britain, the automobile was the brainchild of the United States. Although the United States had a huge length of railway track, it is such a large country that railways were often few and far between. By contrast, railways could serve most places in Europe, and there was less need to find another means of transport. So while Europe had hardly begun to produce new roads, the United States had, by 1921, planned the development of a national highway network and by 1930 had over twenty million vehicles on its roads. In contrast, Europe, Australia and most other countries of the world first used motor vehicles for public transport (trucks and buses). Private vehicles only became common in Europe in the 1950s and, along with motorcycles, have only become common in the developing world in the 1980s.

> The motor car was a success because huge numbers could be built cheaply by mass production methods.

Flight

Flight has brought the places of the world much closer together. Like the steam train and the motor vehicle, flying has developed exceptionally quickly because it provided the fast long-distance transport that had never been available before.

At the beginning of this century it was still unthinkable that people would ever travel

The development of air routes

The first air routes were established not by aircraft but by large propelled balloons – airships. These began flights in Germany in 1910. At first they were a great success, carrying over 35,000 passengers between German cities.

Soon aircraft had proved much more suitable for carrying people quickly and conveniently, and in 1919 the first commercial international flight was made between London and Paris.

The ability to travel long distances at high speed was the key to success for aircraft. So the trans-Atlantic flight of Charles A. Lindbergh in 1927 was of great importance.

Most of the first flying was done overland. For transport across the ocean, however, the unreliability of early aircraft meant that it was risky to use a plane that could only land on hard runways. Furthermore, many countries had not built runways in these early days and landing was only possible in harbors and on rivers. For this reason aircraft called "flying boats" were used widely.

In 1939, at the outbreak of World War II the United States airline Pan Am began the first nonstop commercial passenger service across the Atlantic using a Boeing 314 Yankee Clipper flying boat. After World War II the jetliner quickly replaced both the flying boat and the ocean liner as the main way of crossing the North Atlantic.

The importance of flight to Australia
To countries that are sparsely populated, flight proved to be the most important transport revolution. In Australia, for example, it will never make sense to build railways or major highways to the more remote areas. But early on it made sense to adopt flight as a means of getting people around.

The aircraft that came to dominate Australian life until the recent jet age were small light aircraft. A flying strip can be as simple as a patch of mown ground and the expense of track or highway is not needed. A small single-engine aircraft is as cheap as a motor vehicle to buy, so it is admirably suited to connecting farmsteads and small settlements.

Australians were so quick to take on board the idea of flight that they had already begun a regular airmail service in 1914, four years earlier than in the United States, where the aircraft was invented!

Today, flying has been adapted in many ways, from its use by people who commute to work daily or go shopping using their own plane, to the world-famous "flying doctor" service that allows medical aid to reach people living deep in the outback.

❏ (right) One of the many self-employed Australian pilots who operate a short-distance taxi service using light aircraft.

☐ (above) This picture shows one of the earliest flights in the world when a city street could still be thought of as a runway! Claude Grahame-White returning to Washington, D.C., October 10, 1910.

The distance across North America is nearly as great as the distance across the North Atlantic. This is why Americans travel between most of their cities by air.
    Europe, by comparison is small, which is why air routes within European countries are less important.

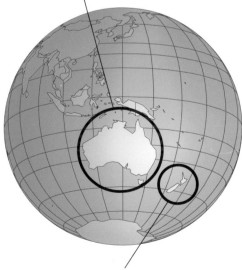

Australia is bigger than Western Europe, and most of its cities are on the coast. Intercity travel is most convenient by air.

Australia and New Zealand are in the "ocean" hemisphere. As a result, travel to other continents is almost always by air.

through the air. But the internal combustion engine was to revolutionize air transport just as it had revolutionized ground transport.

The development of the airplane was extremely rapid. After the Wright brothers' first flight in 1903, fighter planes were already in the air in 1914, during World War I, and commercial air travel began soon after that.

Cheap flights have opened up international travel and are responsible for the ever-growing international tourist industry.

Air travel was particularly suited to large countries and those with sparse populations. In these places air travel soon threatened long-distance railways. Today, flight is the common way of traveling long distances, and the world's major airports handle over fifty million passengers each year.

The cargo revolution

Cargo had traditionally been handled in small amounts because it was handled by people. The revolution in cargo came in finding ways of moving cargoes in bulk.

The oil industry was one of the first to press for bulk movement, because of high railway charges for moving oil in barrels. By the start of the 20th century, therefore, oil was being piped from the oilfields to cities. Today, pipelines carry as much cargo (mainly oil and chemicals) by weight as trucks.

Fifty years later the problem of carrying fragile items in bulk was solved by the use of large steel standard-size boxes called containers. Cargo could thus be fitted exactly onto a truck, a railway wagon or a ship and could be stacked like a pile of bricks.

This has been the most silent revolution of them all.

Containerization

Containers have revolutionized transport because the containers are of standard sizes. This means that trucks, cranes, railway wagons, ships and handling systems can all be designed to take advantage of the standard size, reducing the overall cost. Containers are packed and sealed at the factory, so the contents are less likely to be damaged in transit or to be stolen.

Standard containers are 20 or 40 feet long, 8 feet high, and 8 feet wide. The bigger containers weigh about 5.5 tons but they can hold 35 tons of cargo. The total weight is therefore 40 tons, the greatest weight that can be carried on many highways.

Specially built container ships usually carry between 300 and 2,000 smaller containers or between 150 and 1,000 larger containers. Ships can, of course, carry a mixture of container sizes.

It may take just two to four minutes to unload a container from its transport, where by hand its contents may have taken four men and a crane over three hours. The greater speed means ships can turn around faster in harbor and waste less time tied up.

The world's largest container terminal is at Port Newark and Elizabeth in New Jersey. The largest container terminal in Asia is in Singapore, and the largest in Europe is in Rotterdam (the Netherlands).

❑ (left) Look at any place where goods are being moved in bulk and you will find containers. In this picture you can see containers on railway wagons and also lined up by the side of the tracks, having been brought to the site by truck.

❑ (right) A typical container ship is like a huge empty box in which containers are stacked. The containers that can be seen in this picture are only the ones that are stacked above the deckline. More containers are stacked in the hold.

Container ships are built to standard sizes so that they can carry the maximum number of containers without wasting space.

1 The traditional method of loading and unloading cargo was to use large numbers of men to carry the goods. Each man was only able to carry small quantities of cargo. This was not a disadvantage while labor rates were low, but as wages became higher such enormous amounts of labor were too expensive as well as too slow.

2 The volume of cargo that could be handled was improved by the use of cranes. This meant that fewer dock laborers were needed. But because the cargo still had to be handled after it had been lifted in or out of the ship, the transfer of cargo was still both too slow and too expensive.

❐ (above) Some bulky cargoes, such as coal, cannot be put into containers. Instead, the cranes on the dockside support conveyor belts. These are placed in the ship's hold so cargo can be transferred automatically onto the shore, as shown in this picture of Savona harbour (Italy).

3 The development of containerization has been important for dockers because far fewer are needed than just a quarter of a century ago. Many docks have closed because ships can now turn around faster at the docks and fewer berths are need. There are now hardly any dockside warehouses.

Container-handling cranes

Container storage yards. Containers are brought and carried away by truck or train.

❐ (above) Honolulu harbor, Hawaii.

Chapter 3

Routes

When people travel they have to choose a route. When land is first settled routes are quickly chosen for ease of getting around. Later, as the land becomes more settled, and as new ways of transport become available, new routes are chosen or the old routes adapted for the new forms of transport.

You can see the way this has happened in landscapes throughout the world. The longer people have been traveling across the landscape, the more changes you can find.

We all spend a large part of our lives traveling. Sometimes the journeys are routine, such as going to school, and sometimes they are special, such as going on vacation. A journey might be short and on foot or it may be over thousands of miles by aircraft.

With hundreds of millions of people making journeys at any one time, day or night, there could be chaos unless the journeys are organized in some way. For example, every country has a pattern of roads and ways of controlling the movement of the cars, such as traffic lights and other devices.

A pattern of routes, such as roads, makes up a network. People speak of the railway network, for example, meaning all the tracks and stations. An airline network comprises all the airports the airline serves and the routes between them.

❐ (left) Networks of roads and railways run in and out of a city and encircle it like a giant spider's web. Routes linking cities to one another are the lifelines that allow goods to be moved and people to visit one another. Routes within the city allow people to move between work, home and where they shop.

A route may be easy to recognize in the landscape, such as a footpath, or it may simply be a line on a map, such as a route across an ocean.

Networks often consist of main routes fed by smaller routes. You can compare a transport network to a river system where each small channel connects into the major trunk routes making a network.

A network with many types of route offers choice: for example, people can choose to use the superhighways for fast travel, or they can use the ordinary roads for slower travel; they can use superhighways to get close to their destination and then use minor routes for the final part of their journey.

A route across the land

People have to learn to read the landscape if they are to make good routes. Huge earth-moving machines and advanced engineering skills may have made it more possible to follow a direct route, but engineers ignore the landscape at their peril.

The easiest routes are those that follow the "grain" of the landscape. This means either running a route along a hill ridge, to keep out of the way of marshy river valleys, or following the dry edge of a river valley.

Routes can rarely follow a straight line. Often they need to be constructed along a line that takes account of the natural hazards in the landscape.

It is far harder to cross the grain of the land because then the route must be carried over hills and across rivers and other obstacles. To cross hills many steep slopes will occur (which may make the route impassable for some types of transport) or tunnels will have to be driven through the hills. To cross the valleys routes will have to ford the rivers or expensive bridges will have to be built.

Routes across water

A route over land has many obstacles to overcome, but one of the most formidable is water. Perhaps it is a river that has to be crossed, or a harbor or a bay. Engineers have tried to find the best solutions to crossing water, sometimes choosing bridges, sometimes tunnels.

The bridges that engineers have constructed are some of the world's best-known and beautiful structures. Many are shown on this page. The most famous tunnel to date is the rail tunnel under the English channel between the United Kingdom and France (called the Chunnel).

Japan, a country of many islands, has special problems when it comes to crossing water, and they have built the world's longest bridges. The Trans-Tokyo Bay Highway will be a combination of 2.7 miles of bridges, joined to a 6.7-mile-long tunnel in the center of the bay. A suspension bridge with a span of 1.7 miles is being planned for the entrance to Tokyo Bay. Japan already has the world record for a bridge supported on columns. Its 6.7 miles connect the islands of Honshu and Shikoku.

❏ (below) The Sydney Harbour suspension bridge (Australia).

❏ (left) Transport links require an enormous number of bridges. But these are extremely expensive to build and maintain. The United States, for example, has nearly 600,000 bridges, which cost about $50 billion a year to maintain.

This picture shows a two-lane bridge crossing Lake Pontchartrain to New Orleans.

❏ (right) Many of the oldest bridges have replaced ancient ferries. This has meant that engineers have often had to place a bridge along the line of an established routeway even though this may not be the best site for the bridge. In this picture you can see the way the main road passes through the town and across the bridge.

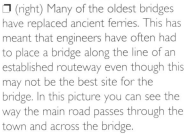

❏ (above) The straits where the open sea and a bay meet are one of the hardest places to build a bridge because the water is usually deep and the currents fast flowing. For this reason many bridges crossing straits, like the Golden Gate Bridge in San Francisco, (shown here), were not built until relatively recently.

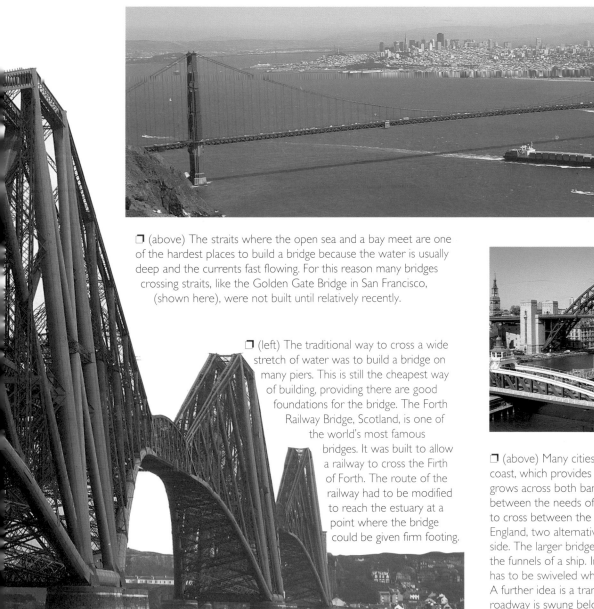

❏ (left) The traditional way to cross a wide stretch of water was to build a bridge on many piers. This is still the cheapest way of building, providing there are good foundations for the bridge. The Forth Railway Bridge, Scotland, is one of the world's most famous bridges. It was built to allow a railway to cross the Firth of Forth. The route of the railway had to be modified to reach the estuary at a point where the bridge could be given firm footing.

❏ (above) Many cities are located on rivers close to the coast, which provides a sheltered harbor. But when a city grows across both banks of the river there may be a conflict between the needs of ships to use the river and of people to cross between the halves of the city. In Newcastle, England, two alternative schemes have been built side by side. The larger bridge is a high-level bridge built far above the funnels of a ship. In front of it is a low-level bridge that has to be swiveled whenever a ship is due to pass. A further idea is a transporter bridge, where a section of roadway is swung below cables and moved from one bank to the other. Only the high-level bridge allows uninterrupted movement of traffic, so although it is the most expensive, it is the most common type built.

Not all land is easy to build on even if it is level. Valley floor land, for example, is flat, but its deep, soft soils may not take the weight of a locomotive or a superhighway and special foundations may be needed. Some land is also liable to slip if cuttings are made, and people using such a route can be faced with hazardous landslides or mudflows.

Routes in river valleys face the extra hazard of flooding after storms of snowmelt and they remain waterlogged and soft for much of the year. Routes that go over high land risk being blocked by snowfall or drifting in blizzards, and routes through deserts risk being covered by drifting sand.

> Networks often contain a few lines for fast long-distance travel as well as a dense pattern for local use.

Most of the ancient routes were produced by hundreds of years of trial and error. People altered the land little. They simply chose a route with the fewest hazards or used one route in summer and a different one in winter. The real problems of building routes have come in the last century when people began to mold the landscape to make more direct routes without appreciating what problems would arise in the years ahead.

Age-old route patterns

The vast majority of routes in the world were established gradually. At first they were no more than well-worn tracks across the landscape; later they were widened and surfaced. Two quite different kinds of route network have grown up in the world. Which kind of route network is near your home depends very much on history.

The first type of network was the result of a gradual spread of settlement. This happened in Europe and Asia. In these continents routes are thousands of years old, and they resulted from generation after generation spreading a little

Crossing mountains

Creating a route across mountains is perhaps the most difficult challenge of all. There are steep slopes and high altitudes to be overcome, but most of all there are problems with the weather.

Mountains are notorious for low clouds, which form fog in travelers' paths, and for the high winds that accompany snowfalls. When the snow melts after a winter of blizzards, there is the extra hazard of avalanches.

All of these hazards require many special measures. Tunnels, although they are incredibly expensive, do overcome the problems of winter snow and fog. They also allow vehicles and trains that would otherwise not be able to climb the mountain slopes to cross mountain barriers. Tunnels have been built on many of the world's most important trading routes, such as under the Alps to connect Italy with northern Europe.

❑ (above and below) The modern solution to mountain travel is to choose a route where a fast highway can be constructed to get as close to the highest peaks as possible. Only the most difficult stretch is made into a tunnel because of the high costs involved.

❑ (right) High mountain passes are usually blocked with snow for over four months each year. This pass in the French Alps is only just being cleared in April. Many of these passes have been replaced with tunnels.

❐ (below) The traditional way of crossing difficult terrain was by pack donkey. This is still the most common way of travel for people crossing the Himalayas.

❐ (left) A country that does not have good routes across the mountains remains backward and poverty stricken. This is a mountain road in Afghanistan that is only passable using a four-wheel drive vehicle.

❐ (right) Mountain passes, such as this one crossing through Yosemite, California may require huge excavations to provide the space for even a normal-sized road. In winter such passes are blocked by snow.

further from the known world and setting up villages or camps. Few were interested in traveling a long distance or exploring the unknown. Most people simply needed to visit neighboring settlements. The route pattern is like a complicated cat's cradle or spider's web of densely packed crisscrossing routes.

Routes of colonization

Rapid exploration produced a very different pattern of routes. The main routes were forged in the Americas, Australia and Africa by exploration. Government officials (such as Lewis and Clark in America) or traders and trappers would try to find routes across wild country. Nobody was settling the land at this time, so these long trails were not made into a network. Instead, people settled along the route that had been explored.

> Route patterns in densely settled land crisscross randomly, whereas routes of sparsely settled lands are more like a grid.

In this way many parallel routes were developed, but the land between remained sparsely settled. Later, when there were more people to settle the land, smaller link routes were built to connect the early settlements. The route pattern that this type of history gives is gridlike, and the settlements are quite spread out.

In America and Australia, routes have eventually become connected, although there are still very few connections through the open dry plains and deserts. But in South America and Africa, few transcontinental routes have been made because the continent is divided up into many countries. Explorers went inland but did not attempt to link up with neighboring territories (with whom they were often in competition or at war).

The lack of international route connections has been one of the single most important factors in holding back the development of

Routes for newly settled lands

Routes tell us about the way people settled their lands. In areas where settlement has occurred since ancient times, such as in the United Kingdom, France or China, a dense network of routes developed. It was designed to connect all the settlements together in a kind of cat's cradle pattern.

The way new lands are settled is very different. Some colonies, for example in Africa, were approached from the sea. The first step was to find a sheltered harbor and set up a permanent settlement. Trade followed and new settlers arrived.

Soon, people began to explore inland. They were often encouraged by government officials who wanted to know about any riches that could be found. To do this a few routes were made into the interior and trading posts and forts set up along the way. Only later were some of these main routes linked together as you can see in the diagram at the bottom of the page.

The United States, uniquely, shows examples of both patterns, because the East was developed slowly before the rapid exploration of the West in the 19th century.

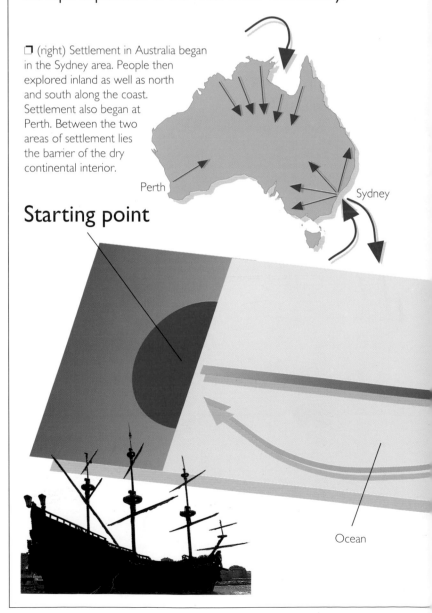

❐ (right) Settlement in Australia began in the Sydney area. People then explored inland as well as north and south along the coast. Settlement also began at Perth. Between the two areas of settlement lies the barrier of the dry continental interior.

Perth

Sydney

Starting point

Ocean

The wagon trains that crossed North America in the middle of the last century followed the overland trail from Missouri to the Pacific Coast.

Columbia River

Independence, Missouri

Oregon Trail

Mississippi/Missouri River system

The first part of the journey from the populated East was by ship and riverboat.

Oregon Trail

The Oregon Trail is a famous trail followed by tens of thousands of Americans seeking a new life in the western United States during the 1840s. It was over 2,000 miles long, beginning at the town of Independence, Missouri, and stretching across the Rocky Mountains and the Cascade Mountains and Sierra Nevada to the valleys of California, Oregon and Washington near the Pacific coast.

The route was chosen so that it could pass through the Rocky Mountains at South Pass and then to the Columbia River. The river was then rafted, completing the journey through gorges in the Cascade Mountains.

The trail was discovered by explorers and fur trappers in the early years of the 19th century. Their reports, and offers to guide prospective homesteaders through the mountains, caused over a thousand people to make the six-month journey in 1843. Many thousands more followed in later years. The route is now indicated by markers and is a National Historical Trail. Modern roads and railways do not follow the old route because it goes over very mountainous terrain.

❐ (below) This rough and ready shack was built by the trappers you see in the picture. As they explored the interior of the United States they gradually made trails and thus unwittingly helped to open up the land for future settlement. These trappers were still opening up the mountainous West at the beginning of the 20th century.

❐ (above) Fording a river in South Africa with traction engines, 1900.

❐ (below) This diagram shows how most colonies were settled and how their route networks built up.

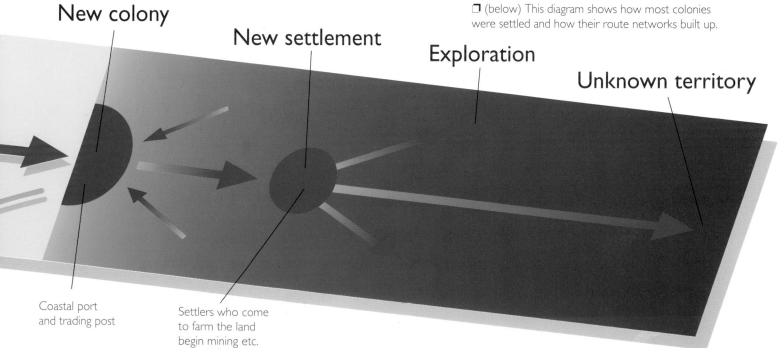

New colony

New settlement

Exploration

Unknown territory

Coastal port and trading post

Settlers who come to farm the land begin mining etc.

both Africa and South America. In each of these continents nearly all routes still run inland from the coast and there is almost no cross-border traffic. Without a network of rail and road links to allow easy trade, inland regions on these continents simply do not develop. At the same time, because the networks keep each country so isolated, they stop different peoples from mixing with each other.

Changing routes

Many traditional routes do not suit our modern way of living. But can we do any better today?

Modern route planners are fitting new routes into a landscape that is already crisscrossed by

> Of all the changes that can be made in a city, route changes are the most difficult.

routes that have been made by people over many generations. A new route is not easy to build without disrupting the way of life of many people, and old routes are not easy to change.

Route changes are particularly difficult in cities. If you want to change the line of the route in a city, then it may be necessary to tear down many buildings, a costly and often unpopular exercise. If the route runs high above street level, then it is also unsightly.

City routes

In a city the main needs are to allow many different activities to go on together. For example, residential areas should be quiet and have no through routes. Industrial areas, on the other hand, need wide, fast roads. Inevitably compromises have to be made because even a residential area has to be connected to major routes so that neighborhood traffic can get to other parts of the city easily.

The main city problems are created by the ebb and flow of commuters from the suburbs

Linking route networks in cities

Routes have one main purpose: to make travel easy and quick. In modern cities roads are often congested because people are traveling by car.

Cars are used because public transport is less convenient. Difficulties include no parking areas near bus stops or railway stations, too few buses and bus timetables that do not link with the railway timetables so that people are left waiting around on platforms or at bus stops.

The only way to persuade people to leave their cars and use public transport is if it is more convenient to use public services than cars and if the transport and parking areas are safe.

Many cities have tried to develop routes that give priority to public transport. In some cities there are bus-only lanes that make it easier for buses to get about in rush hours. Other cities have made sure that the timetables of trains and buses are linked, that buses wait at railway stations and that there is plenty of parking.

Unfortunately, people have lost the habit of using public transport, and more shops and offices are moving out of the city, where it will be difficult to provide public services. This makes it doubly hard to find good public networks that people will use.

❏ (below) A suburban train system works best when it arrives at convenient places. This is a station inside an office complex in Frankfurt (Germany).

Suburban trains that run to the city center and connect the suburbs.

A main railway line that connects to suburban railways and bus systems at a central station.

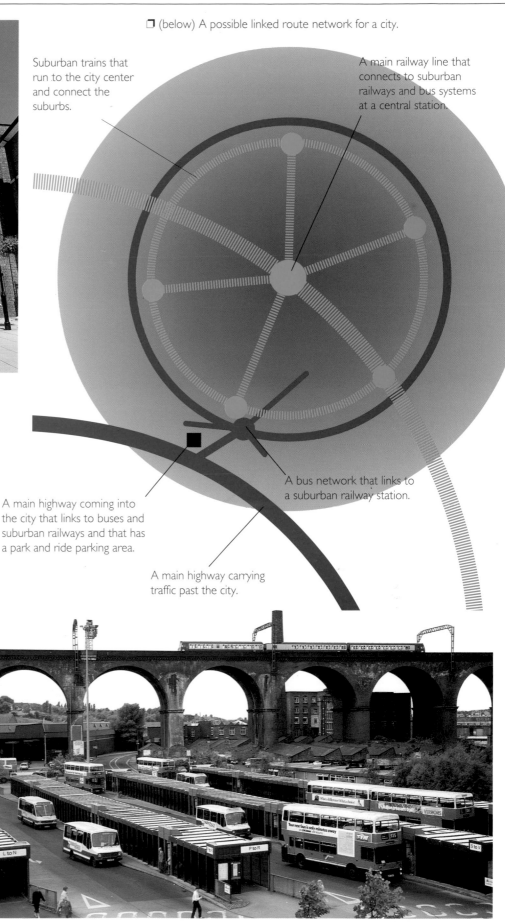

□ (above) Many cities have discovered that the route network in the center can never be made suitable for road traffic yet still allow people to walk about in a safe and healthy way. For this reason many centers have been made pedestrian zones. When this is done, parking needs to be provided close to the center.

A bus network that links to a suburban railway station.

A main highway coming into the city that links to buses and suburban railways and that has a park and ride parking area.

A main highway carrying traffic past the city.

□ (above) Public transport systems have to be conveniently linked to make a city network useful; in old cities this can be difficult. Here, the bus station, which is conveniently next to a big shopping center, is on a completely different level from the suburban railway.

to the center of the city each day. It is very hard to design networks that will not cause traffic congestion unless the roads are made so wide that they take up an unreasonable amount of city space.

Trucks are easier to deal with because their journeys are less complicated. They do not need to go into the residential areas at all. Often a truck route will therefore cross a suburban region as an expressway to make sure that the heavy traffic does not clog up the residential roads.

Improving city routes

The main driving force behind modern change is the incredible growth of the car. In the industrial countries the number of vehicles on the roads is increasing fast, as more and more people choose personal travel and as families choose to have more than one car.

If roads cannot be altered and widened easily, then the increase in traffic in cities cannot be met efficiently. Many schemes therefore aim to make people think of using public transport more often. They do this by reducing parking on roadsides and by charging high fees for parking areas.

Another successful scheme is to discourage through-traffic from using residential streets by closing some roads and making progress slow. This also has the effect of making the streets safer. Safety can be improved even more by forcing the traffic to slow down either by using speed bumps across the roads or by making some parts of the roads narrower.

There are positive ways to encourage more use of public transport, too. By giving buses their own exclusive lanes, public transport can move quickly even when the city is snarled with private vehicles. Some public routes even run against the traffic, giving shorter and faster public transport links. Many city planners are now trying to make more use of streetcars because these can carry people more efficiently than buses.

City road patterns

❏ (above and below) The planned city almost always has a rectangular, or gridiron, plan. Ideally, this should spread out the traffic and reduce congestion. In practice the huge number of traffic lights needed for such a city plan cause congestion every bit as bad as in an unplanned city.

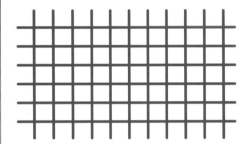

Gridiron route pattern

❏ (below) Most cities that were not planned (and even some that were) have road patterns that spread out from the center and are linked by cross-routes. In some cities the plan is almost exactly like a spider's web, although usually it is more irregular.

Because the main roads come together at the center, there is a likelihood that congestion will grow worse toward the center.

Radial route pattern

□ (right) Trying to improve the traffic in older cities is very difficult. In this example an improvement scheme has been introduced near the center of the city. You can see it as a pattern of divided highways.

The planners have tried to fit the new, faster road inside the old housing pattern, so the final road is a compromise between the most efficient route and the need to destroy many old city buildings. Notice how there has been an effort to reduce the number of junctions. In effect it is a motorway at street level. Unfortunately, such a road is almost impossible for pedestrians to cross.

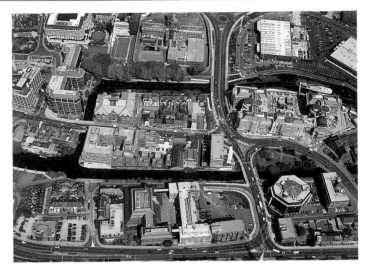

□ (below) In some cases, planners feel that a modern road system simply cannot be fitted into the existing road network. They then try to make improvements by building high-level roads that go completely over the older roads and buildings. Many people regard this solution as worse than the problem.

Chapter 4

A guide to world transport

Today there is a wide choice of methods of transporting goods (freight) and people. The choice is affected by price, comfort and time.

Each type of transport can find its own place in the market, but the competition between carriers and transport makers is more cutthroat than almost any other industry. This chapter will describe the current state of competition.

Railways

Of all the forms of transport in the world, more people have an attachment to railways than any other. The age of the railways is linked with the great Industrial Revolution, a time when nations were building at a tremendous rate and when the steam train was the lifeblood of the nation.

Now, in the industrial world at least, steam trains have been replaced by the less glamorous diesels and electric locomotives, and the railways in the industrial world are having to find a smaller place in a competitive world. However, this is far from true in the developing world, where the railway is still the main transport workhorse.

Modern railways face severe competition, from motor vehicles for short journeys and from

(left) Transport is a matter of being as economical as possible. This picture shows perhaps the ultimate efficiency in carrying goods by cart.

aircraft for long ones. Passenger networks felt the squeeze first, but gradually large trucks and then pipelines were built to carry cargoes more conveniently or more cheaply than the railways. As a result, railway networks are smaller than they were at the beginning of the century.

The decline of the railway has been greatest in the United States. In Africa and Asia railways have not been replaced by roads, and in countries with good networks, such as India and China, they are still the most common way of traveling.

Major railways of the world

There are still 180,000 miles of working railway track in the United States – more than in the whole of Europe. However, intercity passenger travel is now almost entirely by air. The federal government now subsidizes the main passenger service known as Amtrak.

Freight continues to be important on Canadian lines, carrying cargoes from the prairies to the ports. Canada still has 63,000 miles of track, operated in part by the Canadian National Railways and by the private Canadian Pacific Railway.

Railways are now used for travel between nearby cities, for commuters and for bulk cargoes.

In Latin and South America the largest railways are operated in Mexico, Argentina, Brazil and Chile. Nearly all of these lines begin at coastal ports and connect to points in the interior. Brazil's coastal cities are also connected by rail, making Brazil's railway system the best in Latin America.

In Western Europe trains still play an important role in intercity travel. Europe's intercity trains are, along with those of Japan, the fastest in the world. Recent developments include the railway tunnel under the English Channel (called the Chunnel), which allows

Landmarks of world railways

At their maximum, in the first years of the 20th century, there were about 1 million miles of track worldwide. At this time nearly every country in the world had at least a short length of track connecting cities or mines and ports. Today, only about .8 million miles of track remain, most of it in North America (about 35%), then Europe (35%), Asia (12%), South America (8%) and Australasia (4%). But the track is far less intensively used than in the past, and many people say that the railways are in decline. However, this does not mean the railway is finished, just that it has to settle into a role along with the other forms of transport.

Once, railway owners were determined to make everyone want to use the railway, so they concentrated on providing suburban services with low fares. Today, suburban train travel is still the way the majority of people commute daily in and out of most of the world's big cities.

In North America the railway offered the chance to develop the interior of the continent. Wherever the railway went towns sprang up and prospered. And because the railway was first on the scene, it strongly influenced the pattern of cities.

Asia and Africa were largely colonial lands when railways were introduced to bring valuable minerals, fuels and agricultural produce from the inaccessible interior to the coast. Except in India, there was little attempt to link cities. This is why Africa has virtually no lines connecting its many countries. It was, and remains, a major handicap in the development of the continent.

Japan

Railways in Japan are subsidized very heavily. They link all of Japan's major cities and the four main islands. The 716-mile-long high-speed rail line using the *Shinkanzing* (bullet train) began in 1964 – with trains able to travel at 170 mile/hr. It links Tokyo with other cities such as Yokohama, Nagoya, Kyoto, Osaka, Okayama, and Hiroshima. The railway takes 90 percent of Tokyo's commuters and handles 35 million passengers a day. A bullet train leaves Tokyo Central station every three and a half minutes. An 5,900-mile-long super-express railway is now being built.

Canadian Pacific Railway

The Canadian Pacific Railway is a privately owned railway in Canada. It was completed in 1885, linking Halifax, Nova Scotia, in the east, with Vancouver, British Columbia, in the west. The system extends over 15,000 miles of track.

United States transcontinental railway

The transcontinental railway in the United States was completed in 1869, when the tracks of the Union Pacific joined those of the Central Pacific at Promontory Point, Utah.

The railway companies were given land grants along the entire length of the track and cheap loans to help build it. Much of the railway was built using Chinese and Irish labor.

By 1883 the Southern Pacific had reached New Orleans and Los Angeles, the Santa Fe railway had connected Chicago to Southern California and the Northern Pacific railway had built a line from Duluth to Portland.

Europe

European railways have developed fast intercity services using the world's fastest trains. Most countries have passenger trains that will travel at over 125 miles an hour.

The Canadian Pacific Railway

United States transcontinental railway

The Trans-Siberian Railway

Trans-Andean Railroad

The Indian-Pacific railway

China

Most long-distance travel is by train. Steam trains are still used widely; China is the only place left in the world where steam trains are made.

Trans-Siberian Railroad

Siberia is a region of bog and forest land in Arctic Russia. It experiences very cold, harsh winters.

The railway was begun in 1891 and completed in 1916. It is the longest continuous rail line in the world. This gave Russia a new transportation route across Asia.

More recently the network has been extended and electrified. Nevertheless, it remains a slow way to connect the cities of this vast country. The fastest train to make the 5,735-mile journey takes eight days.

A 2,000-mile parallel rail line, the Baikal-Amur line, is now being built through northern Siberia.

Australia

The Indian-Pacific railway stretches from Perth (on the shores of the Indian Ocean) to Sydney (on the shores of the Pacific Ocean). The 2,400-mile journey takes 65 hours. On its way, the train crosses the treeless Nullabor Plain, which is the world's longest stretch of straight railway track.

Trans-Andean Railroad

The Trans-Andean Railroad runs between Chile and Argentina across the high Andes of South America. The line was built in 1910 from Santiago (Chile) across the Andes to join the rail system of Argentina. The line was electrified in the 1950s.

India

Trains continue to be of central importance. Most are working far beyond their design capacity. For example, the trains running into Bombay station are designed to carry 1,700 people but each train currently carries 3,000 and helps bring the 2.7 million commuters into and out of the city each day.

people to get from the center of London to the center of Paris in half the time it takes to use aircraft.

Russia, so like North America in having huge distances between cities, still relies heavily on its railway rather than on air links. Private automobiles and major highways are few and far between, and air travel is too expensive for the majority of Russians. Russia carries more freight per mile of track than any other country in the world, and it carries the second largest number of passengers (after India).

In Japan cities are close together, just as in Western Europe, and trains are still an extremely important means of travel. Japan is famous for the record-breaking bridges and tunnels that have been constructed to allow railways to connect the larger islands.

Most Japanese people commute by train, and many trains are greatly overcrowded. For the rush hour periods each station has special employees whose job is to push people into the carriages so that the doors can be closed.

In India, as in China, trains are the most important means of travel, with bookings so heavy that sometimes seats have to be reserved several months ahead of travel. Most Indian and Chinese trains run slowly, and with such long distances to cover many journeys take days to complete.

Very few of Africa's railways are connected. South Africa has the largest railway network in Africa, with about 13,000 miles of track connecting the major cities, ports and mining districts. Elsewhere tracks consist mainly of

> Railways continue to be the most important means of travel of most developing world countries, but elsewhere their main role is for intercity and commuter traffic or for freight.

Mass transit for the city

There are many ways of getting people around quickly in a city while separating them from normal street traffic. Here are some of the more popular schemes in the world.

Light railways

Light railways are railways consisting of two to ten cars that run on electricity and do not have a separate locomotive. Many are elevated railways (sometimes just called *el*) designed to carry people around the city on a track built above street level.

New York City had hard rock to tunnel through. Its first light railway, which opened in 1868, ran on a track supported by steel columns.

Most light railways are powered by electricity drawn from a third rail running alongside the tracks. Speed is controlled by regulating the amount of electricity reaching the motor.

Elevated light railways can be unsightly. Many people feel that the older ones, such as those in Chicago and New York, are particularly ugly and noisy. Newer ones, such as London's Docklands Light Railways, have overcome most of the traditional problems.

❐ (below) The monorail system in central Sydney (Australia) was opened in 1987.

(right) The London Underground, the world's oldest underground railway system, was opened in 1863.

(left) The Docklands Light Railway System, London (UK), as it approaches Canary Wharf, the largest new office development in Europe.

Monorail systems

In these systems, which began to be built in the 1960s, the train is supported by one rail. In the saddlebag type, such as that used in Sydney, the train straddles a large rail on which the wheels run. Another set of wheels press on the side of the rail to keep it on track. In 1962 a monorail system was built to connect the Tokyo airport to the city's central business district.

Underground railways

Underground railways (subways or metros) are light railways that carry people below the surface of the ground. In this way it does not provide an ugly obstruction to people in the street, and it does not get in the way of city buildings.

You might think that this is an ideal system, yet it is extremely costly and best suited to parts of the world where the rocks under a city are soft, such as London, Mexico City, Paris, Berlin and Calcutta. If tunnellers have to work their way through hard or waterlogged rocks, such as in Rotterdam, then the costs can be astronomic.

One of the most recently built systems is the Bay Area Rapid Transit (BART) system in San Francisco, yet this can carry only 200,000 passengers daily, a fraction of the London, Paris, Moscow and Mexico systems that carry millions daily.

(below) The hanging railway system, Wuppertal (Germany), opened in 1901. It runs over a river to save space in the city.

unconnected segments of railway, many built from coastal ports by the colonial powers. The most important railways are those in Egypt (Alexandria, Cairo, Nile Valley); Kenya (Mombasa, on the coast) to Nairobi and Uganda; and the Tazara railway from Zambia to the coast of Tanzania at Dar es Salaam.

Australia's first railways were begun in 1854. Much of it was built through hot desert. Today its 27,000 miles of track makes Australia's rail network one of the world's largest.

Roads for intercity traffic

Throughout the world, roads are the most common means of carrying people and goods over relatively short distances. The success of motor transport dates from the discovery of portable sources of power such as internal combustion and diesel engines.

Intercity expressways used to be built with military needs in mind. Today they are mainly used by commuters driving from their homes in the countryside.

Military experts have had a great influence on building national networks. For example, Napoleon, who was once dictator of France, organized the building of a national network of roads for use by his army. These are still the main (arterial) roads of the country and are called the *Routes Nationales*. Each road leads out from the hub of the network at Paris to produce a pattern like the spokes of a wheel.

In the 1920s dictators in Italy and Germany were keen to move armies quickly, and they, too, developed major military road networks. However, these were designed not only to provide the shortest distances between places but also to allow traffic to move quickly. These were the first expressways.

Building roads

Old roads were made of gravel and soil built on a foundation of stone rubble. This made roads strong and durable, but the surface was dusty in dry weather and muddy during wet weather. In the 19th century, asphalt, a petroleum product, was used to seal the surface. However, at first the smooth asphalt was very slippery in the rain. To correct this problem a mixture of chippings and asphalt is now laid on all roads. The chippings make the surface rough and help prevent slipping.

Roads are built so that the minimum of earth needs to be moved. However, motorways have to be built along direct routes between cities and, rather like railways, the routes often need to be cut through hills and embankments or bridges must be built to span valleys. All of these extra features add greatly to the cost of road building.

Modern roads are built using huge pieces of machinery, such as graders, to do the work that previously would have taken many thousands of workers when the tools used were simply spades and shovels.

❑ (below) City motorways can only be built if buildings are demolished. In fact, city motorways break up the city far more than railways, separating the people in one part of a city from another by a concrete wasteland.

❑ (right) The United States has the world's largest length of all-weather surfaced roads, with just over 4 million mile. The countries with the densest networks of roads are Belgium and the Netherlands.

❑ (below) Modern cars are designed to run on smooth road surfaces. Older cars had higher ground clearance to cope with rutted tracks.

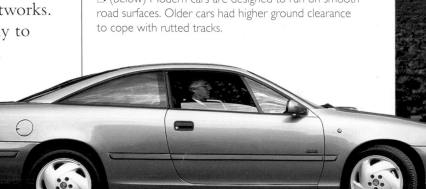

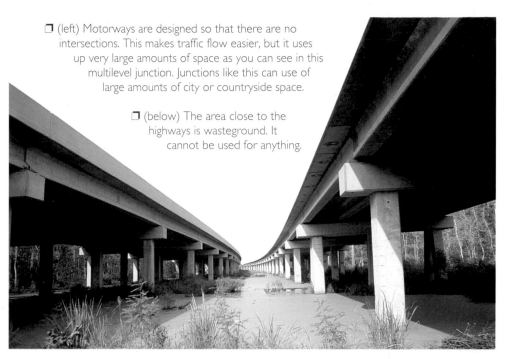

☐ (left) Motorways are designed so that there are no intersections. This makes traffic flow easier, but it uses up very large amounts of space as you can see in this multilevel junction. Junctions like this can use of large amounts of city or countryside space.

☐ (below) The area close to the highways is wasteground. It cannot be used for anything.

The first Italian expressway (*autostrada*) was opened in 1924. The German expressway (*autobahn*) network was designed to remove the problems of traffic jams that plagued ordinary road systems. The *autobahns* were modeled on the railways, with flyover junctions (or overpasses) to connect roads, rather than direct crossings. Germany had over 1,300 miles of *autobahn* at the start of World War II.

Americans were not interested in expressways for military purposes or to allow cars to go faster. Rather they were first constructed as part of an attempt to preserve the strips of land near rivers from development. For this reason many major urban highways are called parkways: they literally run through grass and forest land in the heart of cities like New York.

> Long-distance roads can be extremely expensive to build and maintain and are found mainly in the industrial world. In these countries trucks now carry many of the goods that formerly went by rail.

The Great Depression, which took place in the United States during the 1930s, also played a major role in the building of long-distance highways in America. Road construction was seen as a way of providing jobs for some of the millions of unemployed. But it was not until 1956 that the national system of interstate highways was introduced.

In countries such as the United Kingdom, Japan and Australia, the first motorway construction dates from as recently as the 1950s (the M1 in the United Kingdom) and 60s (the Meishin Expressway from Kobe to Nagoya in Japan). Before this time main roads were usually built simply to bypass congested towns and cities.

Trucks and the trucking business

The earliest trucks (lorries) were used in cities only because they were not powerful enough to manage the rough country roads. The truck industry was revolutionized by the need for trucks in World War I.

Trucks now come in a number of sizes. The smallest are called panel trucks, which generally carry less than 2 tons. They make day-to-day deliveries of small amounts of cargo.

The next size is up to about 7 tons. It has very heavy suspension and is designed to carry large loads from one industrial site to another or to deliver bulk goods to shops. It may have an open back, metal sides (like a panel truck) or a frame and fabric sides that are used simply for weather protection.

Larger trucks can pull up to 40 tons. Many of them are articulated, that is, the engine and cab (called the tractor unit) are separate from the load-carrying trailer. These large trucks are usually so long that they would be difficult to manuever unless they were made of two sections. In some countries a tractor unit is allowed to pull two trailers, but these vast trucks are normally banned from city roads and used just for long-distance haulage.

Some of the world's largest trucks are found in the outback of Australia, where they are known as road trains. These consist of a tractor unit and several trailers coupled together. They may reach lengths of up to 260 feet.

❐ (right) Many trucks are now designed to carry containers.

❐ (below) A specialized truck for carrying bulk liquids.

□ (below) This large articulated truck has flexible sides to make loading and unloading easier.

□ (below) A contract truck carrying coal.

Problems of trucks on roads

Trucks are the largest and heaviest vehicles using the roads. They can easily weigh over forty tons, up to eighty times heavier than an automobile. Because they are so heavy they can easily damage roads, crushing the surface tarmac and breaking up the foundations.

Heavy trucks take a long time to reach cruising speed. This means they move very slowly on normal roads that have bends, intersections and traffic lights, and the more slowly they move the more it costs to deliver the goods and the more the goods cost in the shops.

The noise and vibration caused by trucks can also be unpleasant for people living nearby. So for all these reasons most countries try to build special roads for trucks – motorways between major cities and main highways with bypasses around towns and villages.

□ (right) These are large articulated trucks of the United States. The USA has over forty million trucks, and the trucking industry employs about eight million people.

Today, many countries have motorways, and some of the fastest growth in motorways is in newly industrializing countries like Korea, Singapore and Taiwan.

Major highways seem always to be congested. Yet no matter how many lanes are built, the traffic soon increases to fill the space.

Elsewhere the enormous cost of road building has meant that super-highways are limited to short stretches in cities and many grander schemes have never taken off. The Pan-American Highway, designed to link the capitals of all the American states, is still not even close to completion.

City traffic

Of the millions of miles of roadway, just a small percentage is made of express or long-distance highways. Most highways connect streets within neighborhoods or link commuting villages to the nearby cities. In just a few tens of square miles there may be millions of people each trying to get from home to school, work or the shops.

There are more types of transport in a city than in any other place, a sure sign that there is no single best and easiest way to travel.

Buses and streetcars for city streets

Many types of road vehicles are used throughout the world to carry people through the busy city streets. Some are streetcars that run on tracks. These large, heavy vehicles are usually powered by overhead electricity cables. Their advantage is that they are quiet and can carry large numbers of people.

Streetcars have to travel down the center of the road, and many cities have special regulations that make all other traffic stop when a streetcar has stopped. This is to allow people to get on and off safely.

Trolley buses were used in most cities until about 30 years ago; they are used in some cities today. These are buses powered by electricity from an overhead cable, just like a streetcar. The power is taken from a spring-loaded post (called a trolley) that is fitted on the roof of the bus. The trolley touches the cable and draws electricity from it to move the bus. Trolley buses are quiet and can accelerate faster than diesel buses. They do not pollute the streets. As with streetcars, the wires are ugly and the trolley often comes out of contact with the cable. Nevertheless, it is likely that trolley buses will become more popular in the future as pollution control becomes more of an issue.

Buses, either single- or double-decker, are the most popular form of street transport. This is because they are very flexible and are not restricted to the routes along which cables or rails have been laid. However, buses are diesel powered and pollute the environment like all other diesel vehicles.

❑ (right) One of London's famous red double-decker buses.

❑ (below) "Concertina" bus, with a trailing compartment, designed to allow long buses to get around tight city corners. Rheims (France).

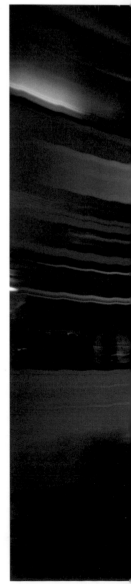

❏ (right) Double-decker streetcars (Hong Kong).

❏ (left) This single-decker bus in New York is part of a network of buses that provide transport in the city center. However, the network does not connect the city with the suburbs as is the case in, for example, European cities. More United States cities are now reviewing their public transport, and some, like Los Angeles, are going back to streetcars.

❏ (right) City streetcar, San Francisco.

Most cities have inherited their problems. Older cities grew at a time when there was no thought of cars or other forms of public transport. Buildings were constructed close together so that people could walk to wherever they wanted to go. Even the older planned cities were never designed to cope with the volume of traffic that they have today. The rush hour, when most people are on the move together, is simply the result of modern ways of working, since most people work the same hours.

> Because of city traffic congestion, cars now move through the average large city at just the same speed as a horse and cart did a century ago!

Shipping

Shipping is the vital link between the world's continents and islands. It has increased dramatically with world trade. The ships have also increased in size, from the merchantmen of the 17th century that could carry 200 tons of cargo each, to the supertankers than can carry half a million tons each. In countries where there are major navigable rivers, inland water transport is also a vital means of transporting bulky goods.

You can usually judge the size of a country by the amount of goods moved on its railway or highway systems. But with shipping this is not always the case. The world's largest fleet (3,500 vessels) is registered to Panama, a small country in Central America. Liberia (a small West African country) also has a large registered fleet.

The number of vessels carrying both passengers and cargo has declined during this century. At the beginning of the century the only way to cross the Atlantic was by ship. However, the rise of the airplane changed all this, offering a crossing in hours, rather than days, and at a lower cost. By 1958 more people

Keeping control of city traffic

The ever-increasing number of cars on the roads of the world's cities makes it important to find ways to smooth the flow of traffic and to persuade people to leave their cars at home or at least to use them more efficiently.

One common way of trying to improve city traffic is to build city highways. Here the idea is to make it easier to get in and out of the city but also to save people living in the city from the noise and congestion of commuter traffic.

Most city centers have parking areas. These are intended to keep parked cars off of city roads so that the whole width of the road can be used for moving traffic. On side roads many cities charge for parking. The idea is to limit the time a car can stay parked so that space will be available for new arrivals.

In residential areas, moving traffic can be a hazard to children. In areas where there is a danger to children from commuters taking short cuts, many devices have been used to deter trucks and fast-moving cars. These include speed bumps across the road and narrowing the road so that trucks cannot get through.

❑ (below) Many cities have extensive one-way systems. In general, more traffic can use a road when all the vehicles move in the same direction.

(left) One way to control traffic is to use urban motorways. In this picture you can see a motor road curving round the shopping center of a city. By providing limited entry and exit points, the motor road is of use mainly to through-traffic, thus keeping local and through-traffic apart.

(below) These huge buildings are for car parking. However, even such massive structures can handle only a small fraction of the number of people who want to bring their cars into a city.

(below) Parking meters are a common sight in city centers. They allow people to spend a short time in the center doing important business. By charging high prices for parking, planners hope that people who do not need to be in the center will be deterred.

crossed the Atlantic by plane than by ship. Today, passenger liners have been reduced to the small number that cruise to destinations like the Caribbean Sea and the Mediterranean Sea. Ferries that carry passengers on short journeys have seen their trade increase as more and more people take their cars overseas. The ferries connecting the United Kingdom and Ireland with mainland Europe, and the Japanese islands with the Philippines, have seen a particularly spectacular rise in trade.

There are now fewer cargo vessels than in the past, but they are bigger. As a result fewer vessels are needed to carry the same amount of goods. Modern ships can travel at higher speeds, and they can be loaded and unloaded far faster than in the past. Shorter turnaround times mean less idle time in dock, and a smaller number of ships can carry the same cargo than in the past.

> Ships carry cargoes between countries. While their numbers have decreased, the amount they can carry has risen dramatically.

Most vessels ply the seas following the same paths, called shipping routes. The busiest shipping routes are between North America (and cities like New York) and northern Europe (and cities like Rotterdam in the Netherlands and Antwerp in Belgium). The Australia/Asia/Mediterranean route, which uses the Suez Canal, connects ports such as Melbourne and Sydney, Tokyo, Hong Kong, Singapore, London and Rotterdam. This route is also well used. Other important routes connect North and South America and Pacific cities with the East Coast of the United States and with Europe, using the Panama Canal.

Modern aviation

Aviation, the operation of aircraft, has been the most dramatic change to 20th-century travel. At the turn of the century most people

Seaborne cargo

Cargo is mainly carried either in bulk carriers or container ships. Bulk carriers designed to transport coal are called colliers. Bulk carriers designed to carry liquids are called tankers. These are the world's biggest vessels.

There are four types of tanker: oil tankers, chemical carriers, liquefied-gas carriers, and OBO (ore/bulk/oil) tankers. There is great concern about oil tankers because they can release such enormous quantities of oil if damaged. The *Exxon Valdez* disaster in Alaska was one such incident.

Oil, which is such an important raw material for the world, is in huge demand. Carriers average 200,000 tons and have been built to hold over half a million tons. Chemical carriers are just a tenth of this size because the cargoes are much more specialized.

The OBO tanker is a combination vessel that can carry liquids or dry materials. These are also giants, averaging 220,000 tons.

A freighter is a general purpose cargo vessel. Many such vessels run on regular schedules and are called cargo liners; others only run on demand, and these are known as tramp ships. Most freighters are small in the league of cargo carriers, able to carry loads of less than 11,000 tons! Container vessels are the newest form of freighter, with capacities of about 16,500 tons.

❏ (above) A container terminus in Singapore.

❏ (above) Coal being unloaded at Port Kembla (Australia).

Inland Shipping

Most continents have large river systems that traditionally have been important for carrying cargo. To the natural rivers have been added canals. For example, the United States and Canada have over 25,000 miles of navigable waterways based on the Saint Lawrence and the Mississippi River systems. In Europe the Rhine and its tributaries carry cargo to the heart of Western Europe; the Volga and its tributaries and the Danube River system are vital to Eastern Europe. China uses the enormous Yangzte and Hwang He River systems.

Most of the cargo in industrial countries is carried by towing barges behind tugboats. In some countries over fifty barges are strapped together and pulled by the same tug.

An alternative way of moving barges is used on narrow waterways. Here the barges are strapped together and pushed upstream, about eight at a time.

Almost all inland cargo is made up of bulky goods such as petroleum, coal, grain, ores and building materials. It is often prepackaged and sent in containers.

❒ (right) Grain being unloaded into an oceangoing ship from a riverside storage site.

❒ (below) Oil being pumped onto a large tanker on the banks of the Mississippi River near New Orleans.

❒ (above) Self-propelled barges carrying chemicals on the Rhine (Germany).

❒ (left) Huge barge clusters being pushed by a tug.

thought it preposterous that they would ever travel through the air in a machine heavier than the air itself. The first international civil aviation service began between London and Paris in 1919, and soon major pioneering airlines, such as Imperial Airways (now British Airways), KLM (Royal Dutch Airways), Quantas (Australia) and Pan-American Airways, had developed.

The aircraft industry soon jumped from a tiny 18,000 passengers worldwide in 1927 to a billion passengers today. This is because people who travel by air have none of the natural obstacles that face those who travel by land or sea, and they need not stop at national frontiers. At 500 miles/hr (the speed of a long-distance passenger jet) people and cargoes can also be whisked over long distances in a very short time.

Airline travel has become the most popular way of visiting countries overseas. It even allows tourists to travel around the world in the space of their normal vacation time.

Few of the pioneering airlines still remain. Most, like Air France, are national carriers, meaning that the airline is partly owned by the government. Airlines in the United States, such as United Airlines and American Airlines, are privately owned.

The growth of aviation in the United States has been particularly dramatic. From carrying just two percent of the intercity passengers in 1939, the airline industry has moved to a position where it now carries nearly 85 percent of all those making intercity journeys.

Modern aircraft are called jetliners, of which the most famous is the Boeing 747, the jumbo jet. There is now a wide range of aircraft to suit all needs. Large aircraft like the jumbo are used only on the busiest long-distance routes. They fly between major airports where

Airports and air traffic

Airports are some of the busiest terminals of all transport systems. Aircraft can wait a short while in the air if there is no space for them to land (a process called stacking), but in general aircraft have to be allowed to land as soon as they approach an airport. This means that huge amounts of space have to be allocated for planes waiting to go to the terminal and also for those waiting to depart.

Airlines operate between countries using international airports. But aircraft need frequent servicing, and airlines must provide hangars and other facilities where the aircraft can be serviced. This expensive service facility cannot be provided everywhere the airline goes, so although airlines can get emergency repairs when away, each airline usually depends on a home-base airport, or hub, where they can get special facilities.

At the homebase the airline also gets priority for taking off and landing, so they use that airport to transfer passengers as they move between destinations.

❏ (above) The real expansion of the airline trade has been due to the rise of tourism. The tourist trade makes up the bulk of journeys to many developing countries.

❏ (above) A modern aircraft can carry hundreds of people. Handling many thousands of people an hour is a major problem for all airports.

(below) An airport requires a large space for runways and so that aircraft can be parked conveniently for the passengers. Here you can see a small part of a large airport. Each plane has been parked against the terminal building. Notice the need for major roads to the airport terminal as well as a large space for car parking. To this must be added all the space that is needed for maintenance and the many trucks and carts that are used in ferrying fuel, food and luggage to and from the planes.

(above) Airports have to handle massive numbers of people while giving each traveler a pleasant time. This is reason airports have a wide range of shops and other facilities.

(below) An aircraft waits for passengers to board. Here you can see the many kinds of service that have to be provided. Everything is designed to work as fast as possible so that the aircraft is on the ground for as short a time as possible.

passengers change to smaller planes to go to the airports of their destination.

In a sense people use airlines like "skytrains." Airports have become like railway stations and are some of the busiest places in the world. The major airlines operate out of hubs, making it easier for passengers to change planes.

Airplanes are mainly used for carrying people, but there is also an important trade in cargo. Aircraft can carry high-value or perishable cargo quickly to its destination. This suits important documents, electronic equipment, fresh flowers and similar cargoes. Major courier companies operate fleets of planes similar to passenger airlines, on similar routes and with regular schedules.

People and animal power

Although more and more people travel around the world using motor transport, the vast majority of those in the developing world must still rely on their own power or that of animals to get around.

A wide variety of means of transport is used in developing world countries. Carts, whether pushed by people or pulled by animals, can still be seen on the streets of many countries. Provided food can be found for the animals, this form of travel is much cheaper than the cost of a truck and its fuel.

❏ (above) A Sudanese steam train, a relic from a colonial past.

Transport mix of the developing world

Transport in the developing world is much more varied than in industrial world countries. You can see the most modern trucks and buses alongside people who are still using oxcarts. This is because the developing world is changing fast, and while some people have been able to make enough money to prosper others have been left behind and cannot afford modern transport at all. On this page you can get a feel for the many kinds of transport and some of the special traffic difficulties that they create.

❏ (left) A cycle rickshaw carrying people.
❏ (below) By using vehicles to their limits, even the less-well-off can share the benefits of transport.

□ (above) The streets of cities in India provide the chance to see more types of transport being used than perhaps anywhere else in the world. Here you can see every kind of transport, from the most ancient to the most modern.

□ (below) People in the developing world are very practical: buses can carry goats as well as people to market!

Bicycles have suited many developing world countries. China in particular saw that its people needed to get around, but that they would never be able to afford motorized transport. So a huge program of bicycle building was started. At rush hours, bikes flood onto the streets, causing just as much chaos as automobiles do in the industrial world.

There are thought to be 500 million bicycles in China alone.

There are other ways to carry people, for example, rickshaws. These are small carts, that are either pulled by a person using long handles or are ridden like a bicycle. They are common in many Asian countries, especially India, Pakistan and Bangladesh. Rickshaws can also be used to double up as freight carriers over short journeys.

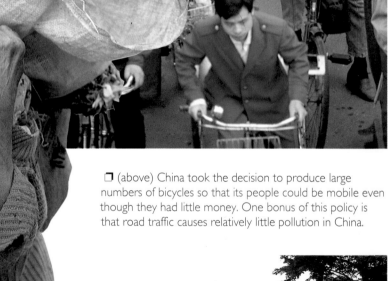

❏ (above) China took the decision to produce large numbers of bicycles so that its people could be mobile even though they had little money. One bonus of this policy is that road traffic causes relatively little pollution in China.

❏ (right and far right) Despite all the advances in transport, money decides whether you must go on foot or if you can have some kind of assistance. The majority of people in the developing world, therefore, go on foot, just as they always have.

Glossary

ACID RAIN
Rain that has absorbed sulphur and nitrogen gases in the atmosphere. These gases are produced when fossil fuels are burned, so all gas-based traffic contributes to acid rain. Acid rain can harm plants and life in rivers and lakes.

COMMUTE
This word is used to mean daily travel to and from a city for work, usually from the outer suburbs or from country places where there is little industry. People who commute are called commuters.

CONGESTION
Congestion occurs when traffic comes to a halt because there are too many vehicles on the roads.

DEVELOPING WORLD
Countries where the majority of people still depend on farming for their living, where wages are poor and there is a lack of advanced technology such as electricity. There are 125 countries classified by the United Nations as coming into this category, including most of those in Asia, Africa and South America.

GREAT CIRCLE ROUTE
The shortest distance on the surface of the Earth. Great circle lines include lines of longitude and the equator.

GREENHOUSE EFFECT
The gradual warming of the atmosphere due to the increase in certain gases such as carbon dioxide. Carbon dioxide is released when fossil fuels are burned, so all gas-based transport contributes to the greenhouse effect.

INDUSTRIAL REVOLUTION
The time, beginning in the 18th century and lasting through the 19th century, when the use of machines became the common way of making goods.

OZONE
A gas that forms close to the ground due to the burning of gasoline. It causes irritation to throat, eyes and lungs and is part of the traffic pollution problem.

SUBURB
A word used to describe the area that makes up the bulk of a city and that contains mostly homes. Most suburbs have grown over recent decades as more people own cars.

Further reading

This book is one of a set that covers the world around us. They may provide you with more information. The set titles are:

1. **People** of the world population & migration
2. **Homes** of the world & the way people live
3. The world's **shops** & where they are
4. **Cities** of the world & their future
5. World **transport**, travel & communications
6. **Farms** & the world's food supply

Index